BEAUTIFUL BRAIDS

by
PATRICIA COEN
&
JOE MAXWELL

Produced by
James Wagenvoord

Prince Paperbacks
Crown Publishers, Inc.
New York

Created and produced by James Wagenvoord Studio, Inc.

PATRICIA COEN

As associate editor of James Wagenvoord Studio, Ms. Coen has contributed to **A Parent's Book; A Lover's Book; The Doubleday Wine Companion; Making Room; The Complete Seafood Book;** and **Beat Insomnia.**

JOE MAXWELL

Joe Maxwell is a hairstylist whose client list has included Elizabeth Taylor, Barbra Streisand, Ginger Rogers, and Ann Miller. He lives in New Hope, Pennsylvania.

Artist–Illustrator—Karen Rolnick
Editorial Assistant—Faith S. Brown
Designer—Carol Hamoy

A Prince Paperback Book

Published by Crown Publishers, Inc.,
201 East 50th Street, New York, New York 10022.
Member of the Crown Publishing Group.
PRINCE PAPERBACKS and colophon are trademarks of Crown Publishers, Inc.

Manufactured in the United States of America.

Library of Congress Cataloging-in-Publication Data
Coen, Patricia.
Beautiful braids.
1. Braids (Hairdressing)   I. Maxwell, Joe.   II. Title.
TT975.C64   1984   646.7′245   83-21325
ISBN 0-517-55222-1

39   38   37   36   35

ACKNOWLEDGMENTS

Linda Biagi, Nisha Biagi, Pat England, Nell Hanson, Karen Kaufman, Terry Coen, Zandy Hartig, Jennifer Hartig, Kumi Tucker, Linda Raglan Cunningham, Maureen Kelly, Linda Hodgson, Lindsay Hodgson, James and Carole Hunt, Lisa Spadaro, Morgan Thomas, Dianne Hughes, Wendy McCurdy, Anita Wagenvoord, Catherine Greenman, Tommy Alessi, Berkey K&L, Marion Zimmer, Laura Woodworth, Lynn Kenny, Karina Kindler.

CONTENTS

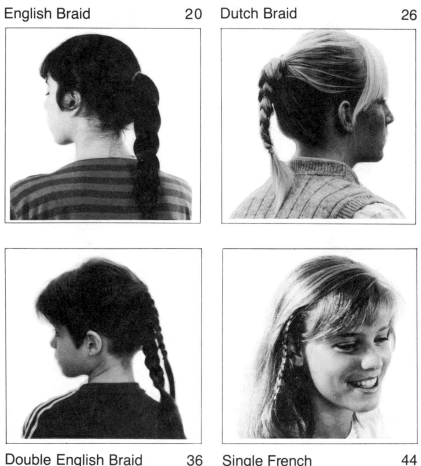

BEFORE YOU BEGIN...

THE BRAIDS

BEFORE YOU BEGIN...

Braids are popular, and they deserve to be. They look good on women of all ages, shapes and sizes. And they're surprisingly versatile. Using easy braiding techniques, you can create literally dozens of elegant hairstyles and looks.

Braids aren't just for long hair. If your hair is chin-length or even slightly shorter, you can use delicate English, Dutch or French braids as accents. If your hair is shoulder-length or longer, you can create any of the braided looks featured in **Beautiful Braids.**

Braids are practical. A properly fashioned braid will stay neatly in place from morning until night, leaving you free to pursue any activity you choose without reaching for a comb. An English braid worn to keep your hair neat during an afternoon tennis match can easily be coiled into a chignon for evening. If your hair is in the process of growing out, leaving you with uneven wisps around your face, you can braid it to keep it swept back. In hot weather, you can fashion any one of a number of braids and pin it up, so your hair will stay off your face and neck.

Although the braided look is as new as today, braids have a long history. In Africa, elaborate braided styles (the forerunners of modern corn rows) were sculpted onto the head

and decorated with beads and precious stones to mark rites of passage for both men and women.

In medieval Europe, long flowing hair was prized as a virgin's attribute. Then, as now, young women devoted hours to pampering their hair with herbs and medications, using combs carved from wood and ivory. Their braids were arranged in a variety of styles—hanging loose down the back, coiled atop the head or curled into braided earmuffs.

Braids retained their popularity in Europe throughout the Renaissance, the styles changing slightly with the times. Braids were wrapped around the head either horizontally or vertically, and small, delicate braids were woven throughout the hair as decoration.

During the Victorian era, braids were arranged to complement that period's demure clothing styles. Braided hair was looped down beside the cheeks and back up over the ears, or coiled in large loops at the back of the head.

Any historical style can be adopted by modern women, along with any of the dozens of braid variations. The beauty of braids is their versatility and simplicity. Once you've mastered a few very basic steps, you can fashion **any** kind of braid, and even begin to create your own styles. Braids are flattering to everyone, and they can be anything you want them to be— innocent, sophisticated, and everything in between.

BRAIDING TIPS

The results of braiding appear intricate, but the techniques are simple. Braiding is a skill that you can easily learn with just a little practice and patience. A few basic techniques, once mastered, will enable you to create both simple and elaborate braids. During your first few attempts at braiding, you'll begin to learn the rhythms of the techniques. Braiding is just the repetition of a simple weaving pattern, and this pattern will soon become natural and comfortable for you.

Visualization is the key to braiding. Before you attempt even one plait, look at the step-by-step instructions beginning on page 13. Imagine yourself carrying out each step on your own hair. Braid your hair at first only in your imagination. Visualization is important even after you begin to braid; as you work, give your complete attention to each step, picturing exactly what the step should look like as you do it and when it's completed. This will keep you from becoming confused as you work.

Don't watch yourself in a mirror as you braid—the reversed image will be misleading. Simply concentrate on what you're doing. Close your eyes to eliminate distractions. When you're finished, check the results in a mirror. Don't be discouraged if there are stray hairs. After you've braided a few times, your touch will become sensitive enough to feel any hairs that are out of place.

Always work with damp hair, or hair that is at least slightly damp. It holds together easily, leaving fewer stray hairs to worry about.

Use a covered rubber band to secure your hair in a ponytail when you try your first braids. Other accessories you'll find useful are clips or barrettes to hold sections of hair out of your way while you're braiding others, and bobby pins or hairpins to anchor styles like the Chignon and the Invisible French braid .

Relax. Many people unconsciously tense their shoulder muscles as they hold their hands up to braid because the position seems unfamiliar. You'll be more comfortable if you avoid this tendency to tighten up.

Keep even tension on all the strands of hair as you braid.

Don't worry about taking the "right" amount of hair for each plait. While the strands should be of about equal thickness to begin with, they needn't be absolutely uniform for the braid to turn out properly.

Take it easy. If you make a mistake, there's no harm done. It will only take a moment for you to unbraid your hair and begin again.

A BRAIDER'S GLOSSARY

Bangs—Hair cut short to fall over the forehead.

Braid—To interlace or entwine; strands of hair that have been interlaced or entwined to form a pattern.

Chignon—Hair gathered and fastened together to give the appearance of a knot or bun. Usually worn at the crown or nape.

Crown—The topmost part of the head. To locate the crown, place the tips of your index fingers above your ears and draw the fingers upward. The point at which they meet on the top rear portion of your head is the crown.

Hairline—The line around the face (temple to forehead to temple) where hair begins to grow.

Nape—The back of the neck, at the base of the hairline.

Plait—One complete step in the braiding sequence, i.e., left over center and right over center.

Sectioning—Dividing the portion of hair you plan to work with from the rest of the hair.

Strands—The sections of hair that are twined together to form a braid. The hair is divided into three strands to fashion a typical braid.

Texture—The characteristic surface of the hair. Fine hair has a different texture than thick hair, and different textures may be suited to different kinds of braids.

FINGER & HAND POSITIONS

The methods you will use to braid your hair are the same techniques used to braid or weave yarn, rope or any other materials. Braiding is simply taking three sections of hair and crossing the outside sections over and into the center. As you work, the sections of hair are interwoven to create plaits.

A braid is composed of a series of simple "cross-take-tighten-return" sequences, using motions that flow naturally from and into one another. A complete sequence takes only a few seconds.

There is no one "right" way to braid. Every braider develops individual finger and hand positions that are comfortable and successful for her. Illustrated here are basic positions that act as a starting place or reference point.

The illustrations show the beginning of an English braid, with your hands in position at the back of your head. Obviously, to fashion a braid on the side of your head, your arms and hands will be placed somewhat differently; that's an adaptation you can easily make yourself after you're comfortable with the fundamentals. Remember, ultimately it's what happens to the hair—not the exact finger and hand positions—that's important.

1. Take the left strand in your hand, between your thumb and first finger. The three fingers behind it are free.

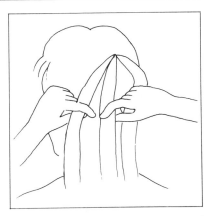

2. Hold the center strand between your right thumb and first finger and the right strand with your last two fingers.

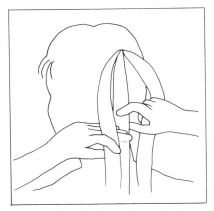

3. CROSS. Cross the left strand over the center strand, holding it slightly above the center strand.

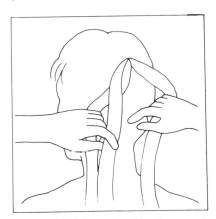

4. TAKE. Loop the free fingers of your left hand over the center strand and take it from your right hand.

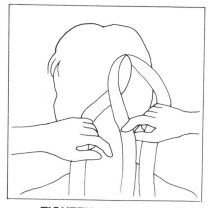

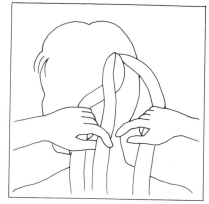

5. **TIGHTEN**. Use your free right thumb and first finger to take the center strand and pull it gently, ensuring that the first half-plait is taut.

6. **RETURN**. Take this new center strand back between the thumb and first finger of your left hand. You're now holding two strands in your left hand and one in your right.

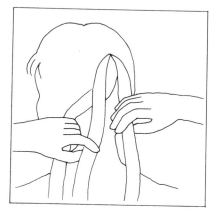

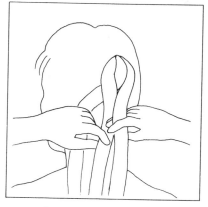

7. Move that strand so that you're holding it between your right thumb and first finger (if you need to let go of the strand to position it properly, go ahead).

8. **CROSS**. Cross the right strand over the center strand, holding it slightly above the center strand.

Now, repeat the "cross-take-tighten-return" sequence, beginning with your right hand.

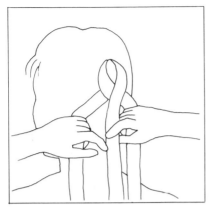

9. **TAKE**. Loop the free fingers of your right hand over the center strand and take it from your left hand.

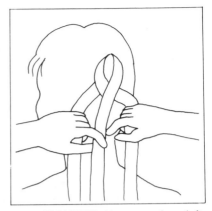

10. **TIGHTEN**. Use your free left thumb and first finger to take the strand and pull it gently.

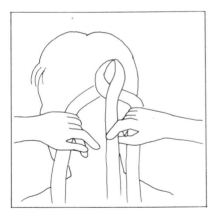

11. **RETURN**. Take this new center strand back between the thumb and first finger of your right hand. You now have two strands in your right hand and one in your left, held by the last two fingers.

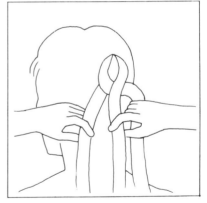

12. Move that strand so that you're holding it between your left thumb and first finger.

Your hands have returned to their starting positions,
except that you now have one plait, the beginning of a braid.

FREEING A HAND

While you're braiding, you'll occasionally need a free hand to smooth the strands you're working with or to make sure a plait feels taut. It's not difficult to hold all three strands in one hand, separated by your fingers. Remember that as you braid, you'll always have two strands in one hand and one in the other. The hand holding a single strand is the one that you should free. These illustrations show a braider freeing one hand.

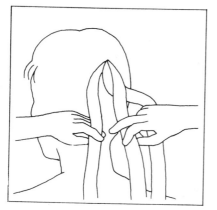

1. Extend the middle finger of the hand holding two strands.

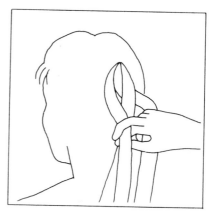

2. Cross the single strand over the center. Curl the middle finger around it, holding it between and slightly above the other two strands.

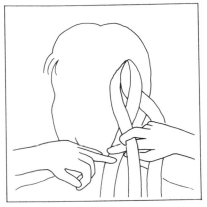

3. To resume braiding, use the last two fingers of your free hand to take the center strand from between the thumb and first finger of your other hand.

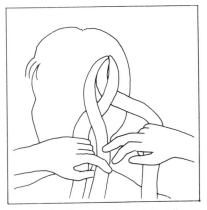

4. Use the thumb and first finger of the hand that you freed to remove the strand held by the middle finger. This makes it the new center strand.

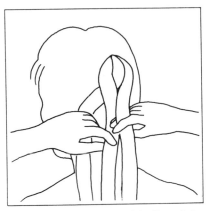

5. You've completed half a plait. Move the single strand from between the last two fingers to between the thumb and first finger and continue braiding.

THE BRAIDS

Every braid, from the simplest to the most complex, is created from the English, Dutch or French braid. Once you've mastered these easy-to-learn techniques, even the most elaborate braid will seem simple. Each technique shown is slightly more advanced (not more difficult) than the one before it, and each braid can stand alone as an attractive style or be used in combination with others. You can use these instructions to braid your own hair or a friend's.

ENGLISH BRAID

The simplest braid is the English braid—the same one that was begun in the **Finger & Hand Positions** section on page 12. This versatile three-strand braid is an element of many different styles. Once you're comfortable with the English braid, fashioning any other braid will be easy.

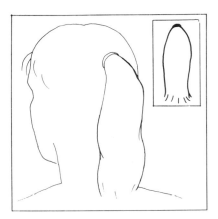

1. Brush your hair back into a ponytail with its base slightly below your crown.

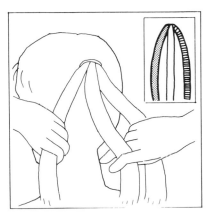

2. Divide the ponytail into three approximately equal strands and position your fingers to begin braiding.

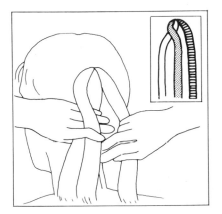

3. Cross the left strand over the center, taking the center strand to the left, so that the two strands trade places.

4. Cross the right strand over the center, taking the center strand to the right, so that these two strands trade places.

ENGLISH BRAID

In your first attempts at the English braid, gather your hair into a ponytail and secure it with a covered rubber band. This will help you keep the base of the braid tightly against your scalp. You'll have to leave the band on after the braid is completed, but you can camouflage it by using a color that's close to your hair color. Or you can coil the braid into a chignon

5. Cross the left strand over the center, taking the center strand to the left.

6. Cross the right strand over the center, taking the center strand to the right.

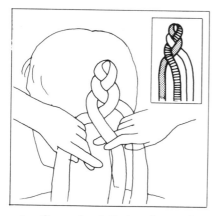 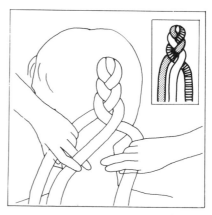

7. Cross the left strand over the center, taking the center strand to the left.

8. Cross the right strand over the center, taking the center strand to the right.

(see page 24) to hide it. With practice, you'll be able to begin a braid neatly without the rubber band, simply keeping the first plait very tight against the scalp to act as a foundation.

As you become more comfortable with braiding, you can modify the techniques shown to find the method that suits you best.

9. Cross the left strand over the center, taking the center strand to the left.

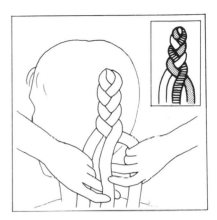

10. Cross the right strand over the center, taking the center strand to the right.

11. Continue crossing the strands alternately over the center, until the braid is as long as you want it.

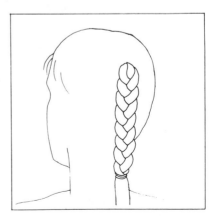

12. Fasten the end with a covered rubber band.

ENGLISH BRAID
WITH CHIGNON

In just a few steps, you can turn the basic English braid into an elegant hairstyle. If you've used a covered rubber band to anchor the base of your English braid, creating a chignon will conceal it. Follow the instructions for the English braid on page 21 and then carry out the following steps.

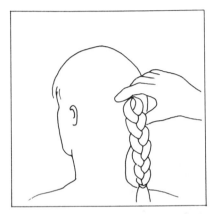

1. Place your index finger against your head, touching the base of the braid.

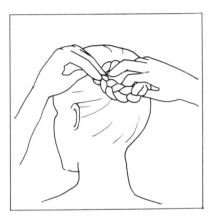

2. Coil the braid around the finger, encircling the base of the braid.

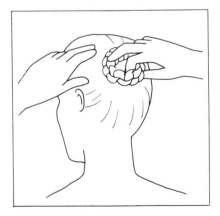

3. Tuck the end of the braid underneath the coil of hair that you've created.

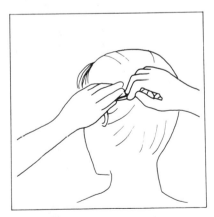

4. Cup the coiled braid in your hand and use hairpins to secure it tightly to your scalp.

DUTCH BRAID

The Dutch braid is essentially a backward English braid. The strands are crossed under, rather than over, the center, so the first plait isn't fitted as closely against the scalp as it is in English braiding. The finished braid appears slightly flat and loose because the plaits are really upside down.

1. Brush your hair back into a ponytail with its base slightly below your crown.

2. Divide the ponytail into three approximately equal strands and position your fingers to begin braiding.

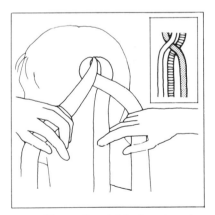

3. Cross the left strand under the center, taking the center strand to the left, so that the two strands trade places.

4. Cross the right strand under the center, taking the center strand to the right, so that these two strands trade places.

DUTCH BRAID

As with the English braid, begin your first few attempts at the Dutch braid with a ponytail anchored by a covered rubber band. You'll be able to give your full attention to mastering the art of crossing the strands underneath one another. You can use the finger and hand positions illustrated on page 12 or devise your own. Once you're comfortable with the braid itself,

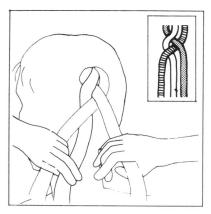

5. Cross the left strand under the center, taking the center strand to the left.

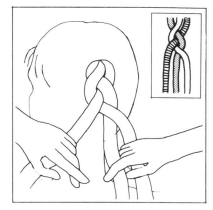

6. Cross the right strand under the center, taking the center strand to the right.

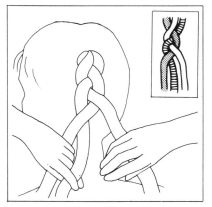

7. Cross the left strand under the center, taking the center strand to the left.

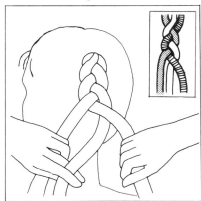

8. Cross the right strand under the center, taking the center strand to the right.

beginning it neatly won't be a problem.

Attractive on its own, the Dutch braid is also an important element of several more elaborate braid styles, including the elegant Underbraid on page 60. It offers almost endless variations and possibilities for experimentation.

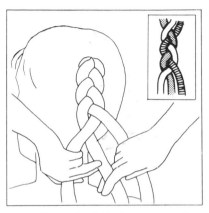

9. Cross the left strand under the center, taking the center strand to the left.

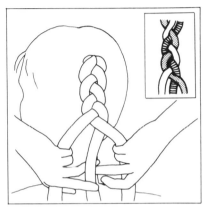

10. Cross the right strand under the center, taking the center strand to the right.

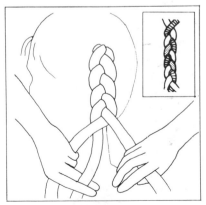

11. Continue crossing the strands alternately under the center until the braid is as long as you want it.

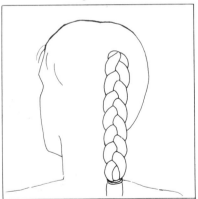

12. Fasten the end with a covered rubber band.

FRENCH BRAID

The French braid, one of the best-known braids, is admired for its elegant, sophisticated look. Its complex appearance is deceiving; it is, in fact, extremely easy to create. It is essentially an English braid with an additional step.

The French braid begins with a thin ponytail skimmed from

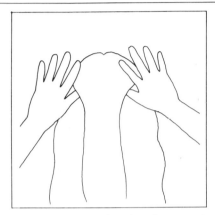

1. Place your thumbs above and behind your ears. Draw your thumbs slightly back and upward, gathering hair that meets at your crown in a ponytail.

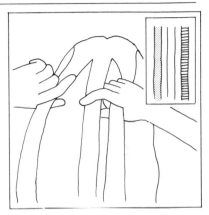

2. Divide the ponytail into three approximately equal sections and position your fingers to begin braiding.

3. Cross the left strand over the center, taking the center strand to the left, so that the two strands trade places.

4. Cross the right strand over the center, taking the center strand to the right, so that these two strands trade places.

FRENCH BRAID

the top layer of your hair. As you braid, you'll gather additional hair and add it to the strands. These additions result in gracefully draped hair on either side of the braid. The appearance of the drape varies with the amount of hair you add and the tension you keep on each strand. Experiment and see what works best for you.

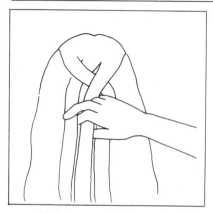

5. Hold the plait in your right hand, separating the three loose strands below it with your fingers.

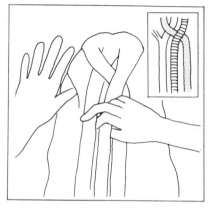

6. Place your left thumb above and behind your left ear. Draw a strand half as thick as one of the original strands toward the ponytail.

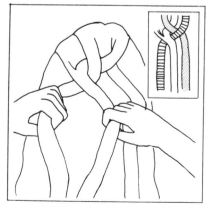

7. Add the newly gathered hair to the left strand. Cross the increased left strand over the center, taking the center strand to the left.

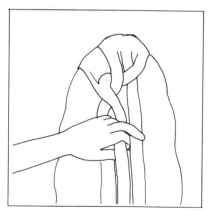

8. Hold the plait in your left hand, separating the three loose strands below it with your fingers.

Visualization is essential to all braiding, but especially to French braiding. Because you're dealing with more than three strands for the first time, the gathering step initially requires your full attention. Read through the instructions once and then perform each step on your own hair, concentrating on how it should look.

9. Use your right thumb to draw a strand of hair about half as thick as one of the original strands up toward the ponytail.

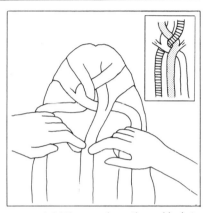

10. Add the newly gathered hair to the right strand. Cross the increased right strand over the center, taking the center strand to the right.

11. Continue gathering hair from the left and right and adding it to the strands just before you cross them over the center.

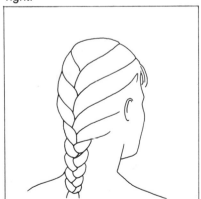

12. After several plaits, there will be no loose hair left to gather. English-braid the remaining strands.

INVISIBLE
FRENCH BRAID

The Invisible French braid is one of the most elegant of all braided looks. Although it's appropriate for everyday, it's also ideal for even the most formal occasion. It begins with a regular French Braid (illustrated on page 30).

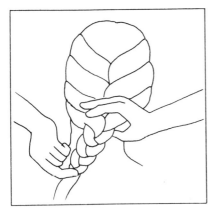

1. Take the hanging, English-braided portion of the standard French braid in your hand.

2. Fold it in toward your neck, tucking it up underneath the French braid, lined up between the gathers.

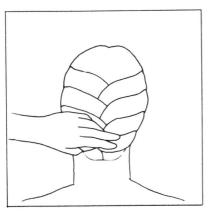

3. The hanging braid is hidden underneath the French braid, against your scalp.

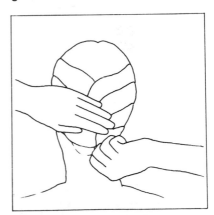

4. Secure the braid tightly to your scalp with hairpins.

DOUBLE
ENGLISH BRAID

Even the most basic braids can be used to create unusual styles. Double English braids (you can also use Dutch braids to create this style) are an excellent example of braids' versatility.

Double English braids use the basic English braiding

1. Place your thumbs slightly in front of and above your ears, near your temples.

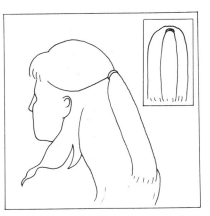

2. Draw your thumbs upward to your crown, gathering the top layer of hair into a thin ponytail with its base at your crown.

3. You'll work with the loose hair first, so secure the ponytail with a covered rubber band and clip it to the top of your head.

4. Divide the loose hair into three approximately equal strands and position your fingers to begin braiding.

DOUBLE ENGLISH BRAID

technique, yet the final effect is very different from that of an "ordinary" English braid. By stacking two English braids, one on top of the other, you can create a unique, casual look.

Like most braids, the Double English braid has its practical side. It is ideal for very thick hair that might pull too

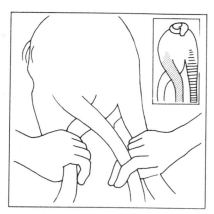

5. Cross the left strand over the center, taking the center strand to the left.

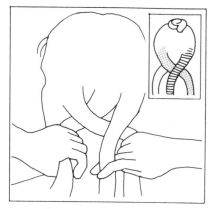

6. Cross the right strand over the center, taking the center strand to the right.

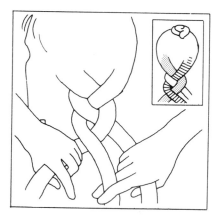

7. Continue crossing the strands alternately over the center. Fasten the end of the completed braid with a covered rubber band.

8. Unpin the top ponytail and remove its covered rubber band.

heavily on the head if it's worn in one braid. However, thick or especially long hair is not a necessity for creating successful Double English braids—you need only shoulder-length hair.

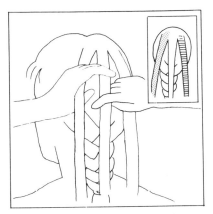

9. Divide the loose hair into three approximately equal strands and position your fingers to begin braiding.

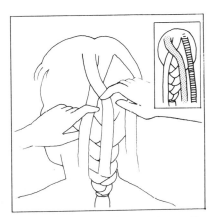

10. Cross the left strand over the center, taking the center strand to the left.

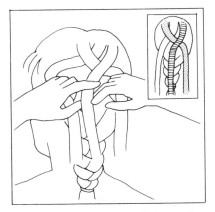

11. Cross the right strand over the center, taking the center strand to the right.

12. Continue crossing the strands alternately over the center. Fasten the end of the completed braid with a covered rubber band.

DOUBLE DUTCH TIEBACK

The Double Dutch Tieback is one of the most practical and versatile of all braids. (You can also use English braids to create this style.) Fashionable and attractive, it has the added advantage of keeping all your hair—both braided and loose—pulled neatly back from your face.

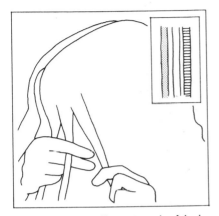

1. Section off a strand of hair approximately ½" in diameter on one side of your face. Divide it into three approximately equal strands.

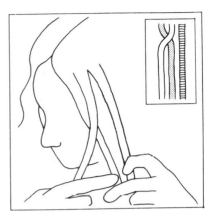

2. Beginning at eye level, cross the right strand under the center, taking the center strand to the right. Pull the strands taut.

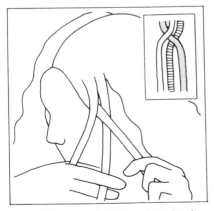

3. Cross the left strand under the center, taking the center strand to the left. Make sure the strands are taut.

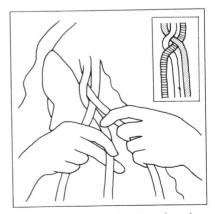

4. Cross the right strand under the center, taking the center strand to the right. Make sure the strands are taut.

DOUBLE DUTCH TIEBACK

Using the basic Dutch braiding technique, you can create a variety of looks by beginning with different sized sections of hair. A very thin section will give you tiny braids that ornament your hair; thicker sections will yield more substantial braids.

The Double Dutch Tieback lets you use your imagination. The braids can be worn loose; you can fasten them with a

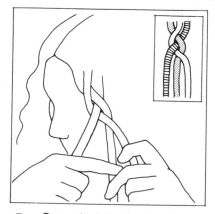

5. Cross the left strand under the center strand, taking the center strand to the left. Make sure the strands are taut.

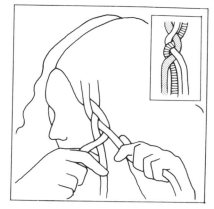

6. Cross the right strand under the center, taking the center strand to the right. Make sure the strands are taut.

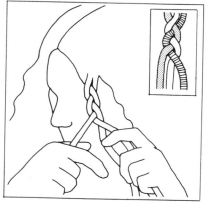

7. Cross the left strand under the center, taking the center strand to the left.

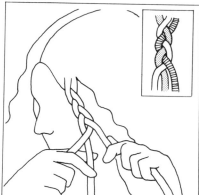

8. Cross the right strand under the center, taking the center strand to the right.

covered rubber band or hair clip; you can pin each one back separately or, if your hair is long enough, you can even knot them loosely together.

The Double Dutch Tieback looks its best when you take care to make the plaits smooth and delicate. Begin braiding on either side of your face.

9. Cross the left strand under the center, taking the center strand to the left.

10. Continue crossing the left and then the right strands alternately under the center until the strands are too short to braid.

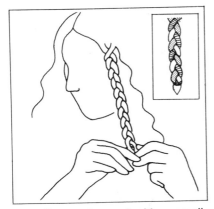

11. Fasten the end with a small covered rubber band. Repeat the steps to fashion another braid on the other side of your face.

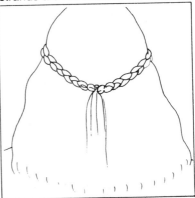

12. You can wear the braids loose, but you'll get a more striking look if you fasten them at the back of your head, sweeping your hair off your face.

SINGLE FRENCH
ACCENT BRAID

The Single French Accent braid is especially easy for the beginner, because you can watch what you're doing as you braid—without using a mirror. Popular with teenagers, the Single French Accent braid gives loose hair a "dressed-up" look.

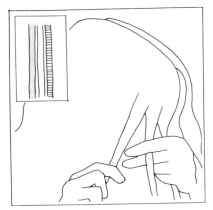

1. Section off a portion of hair about ¼" in diameter right next to your face. Divide the section into three equal strands.

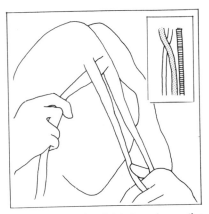

2. Cross the right strand over the center, taking the center strand to the right. Pull the strands taut.

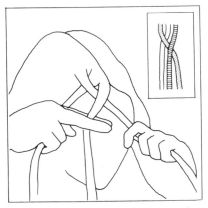

3. Cross the left strand over the center, taking the center strand to the left. Make sure the strands are taut.

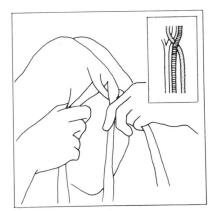

4. Gather a very thin section of hair from the loose hair hanging behind the braid and add it to the right strand.

SINGLE FRENCH ACCENT BRAID

As practical as it is pretty, this accent braid solves the problem of overgrown bangs. Shorter hairs can be woven in with longer ones and held cleanly back from your face.

The Single French Accent braid uses both an English and a modified French braiding technique. You can make the braid as thin or as thick as you like, depending on the amount of hair

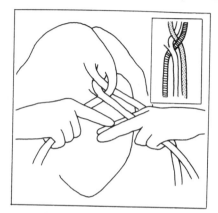

5. Cross the increased right strand over the center, taking the center strand to the right.

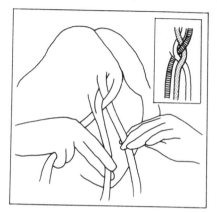

6. Cross the left strand over the center, taking the center strand to the left.

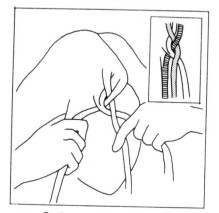

7. Gather another thin section of hair from the loose hair hanging behind the braid.

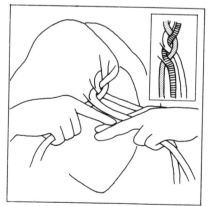

8. Add the newly gathered hair to the right section and cross the increased right strand over the center.

you begin with. The key to a beautiful accent braid is to pull the strands you're braiding extremely tight to accentuate the braid's delicate quality.

You can fashion more than one accent braid and place them anywhere you please. In these illustrations, the braid is being formed on the right-hand side of the face.

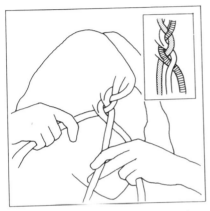

9. Cross the left strand over the center, taking the center strand to the left.

10. Continue gathering loose hair, adding it to the right, and crossing the left and right strands alternately over the center.

11. When the bottom of the braided hair is about level with your eye, English-braid the loose strands below the French plaits.

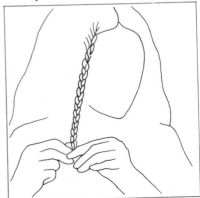

12. Fasten the end of the braid with a covered rubber band. It can be worn loose near the face or pinned back for a more sophisticated look.

BRAIDED FACE FRAME

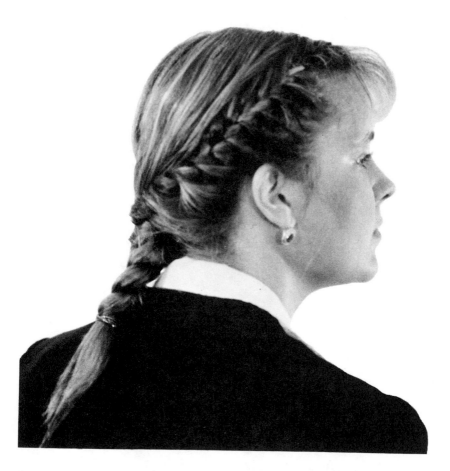

The Braided Face Frame combines two braiding techniques, English and French, resulting in a stunning style that's flattering to everyone. It's also ideal for blending uneven wisps near your face—or bangs that are growing out—in with the rest of your hair, eliminating loose strands.

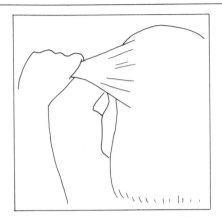

1. Section off a thin portion of hair from your hairline, at your temple. Divide the section into three equal strands.

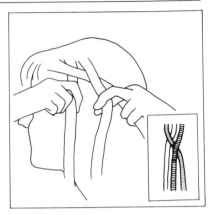

2. Fashion one English plait by crossing the strand closest to your face, and then the one farthest from your face, over the center.

3. Gather a small section (about half as thick of one of the original strands) from the loose hair along your hairline next to the plait.

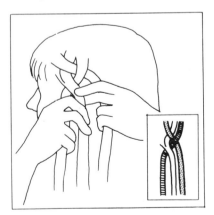

4. Add the gathered hair to the strand nearest your face and cross this increased strand over the center, so that the two strands trade places.

BRAIDED FACE FRAME

The key to fashioning a successful Braided Face Frame is starting it right. Remember to begin your first plait by crossing the strand nearest your face over the center to support the braid from underneath and keep it in place.

You can create several different looks with the Braided Face Frame by experimenting with the amount of hair you

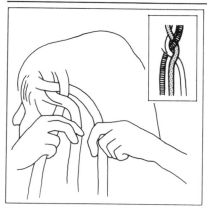

5. Without adding any new hair, cross the strand farthest from your face over the center, so that these two strands trade places.

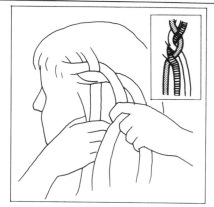

6. Gather a small section of the loose hair next to the braid. Add it to the strand nearest your face. Cross this increased strand over the center.

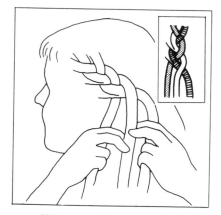

7. Without adding any new hair, cross the strand farthest from your face over the center.

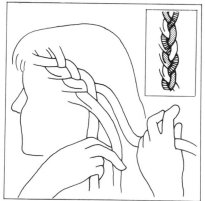

8. Continue adding hair to the strand nearest your face and crossing it over the center, alternately crossing the far strand over the center.

begin with and the thickness of the strands you add. Beginning with a very thin section of hair and adding very thin strands to it will result in a delicate accent braid; beginning with a thick section and adding thick strands to it will encircle your head with a bolder-looking braid.

9. When the braid has nearly reached the nape of your neck, fasten it temporarily with a barrette, hair clip or hairpin.

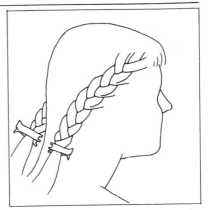

10. Repeat the same steps on the other side of your face, again beginning with the strand nearest your face. You'll have loose hair below the two braids.

11. The unbraided hair between them becomes the center strand of a new braid. Cross the left and then the right strand over the center.

12. Remove the clips. Continue English braiding until the braid is complete. Fasten the end with a covered rubber band.

HAIRLINE TWIST WITH WITH ENGLISH BRAID

The combination of a Hairline Twist with an English braid is one of the oldest and most classic of all braided styles. Slightly formal in appearance, it combines the standard English braid with a twisting technique to create an elegant look that's especially good for very long hair.

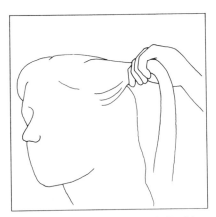

1. Beginning on your left side, section off a strand of hair from your hairline near your forehead. The strand should be about ½″ in diameter.

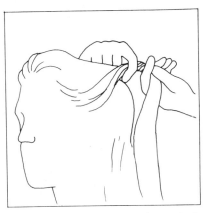

2. Beginning near your face, start to twist this strand up toward the top of your head. Hold it back, not down, as you twist.

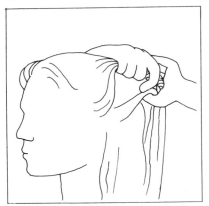

3. When the strand is fairly tight, gather a thin section from the loose hair near the twist and add it to the twisted strand.

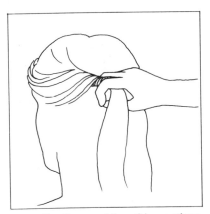

4. Continue adding thin sections to the twist and winding until the twisted hair nearly reaches your nape. Fasten it temporarily with a hair clip.

HAIRLINE TWIST WITH ENGLISH BRAID

The Hairline Twist is a technique that, like braiding, is easy to learn. You begin by sectioning off a portion of hair on either side of your face. Then you wind the section back toward your nape while adding thin strands of hair gathered from the loose hair next to the hair being twisted. This technique gives you a "twist" of tightly wound hair that extends from your forehead to

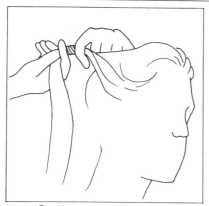

5. Section a strand of hair on your right side. Beginning near your face, twist it up toward the top of your head.

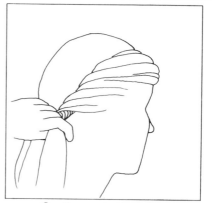

6. Continue winding and adding thin sections to the twist until the twisted hair nearly reaches the nape of your neck. Fasten it temporarily.

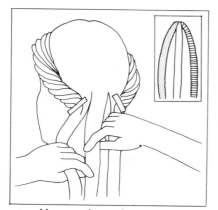

7. You now have three strands— two partially twisted and fastened by hair clips, and one created by the loose, untwisted hair between those two strands.

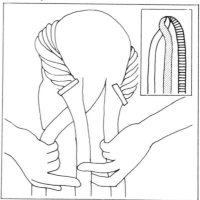

8. Cross the left strand over the center, taking the center strand to the left.

your nape, where it is temporarily fastened with hair clips. Once the twists are secured, you have loose hair beyond the hair clip on each twist, and loose hair in between them that hasn't been twisted at all. These three strands are simply English-braided.

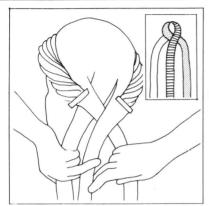

9. Cross the right strand over the center, taking the center strand to the right.

10. You have completed one plait. Remove the clips holding the two twisted strands.

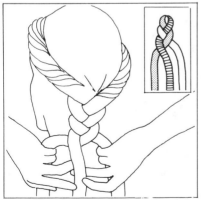

11. Continue crossing the left strand and then the right strand alternately over the center until the braid is as long as you want it.

12. Fasten the end of the braid with a covered rubber band.

FRENCH TWIST

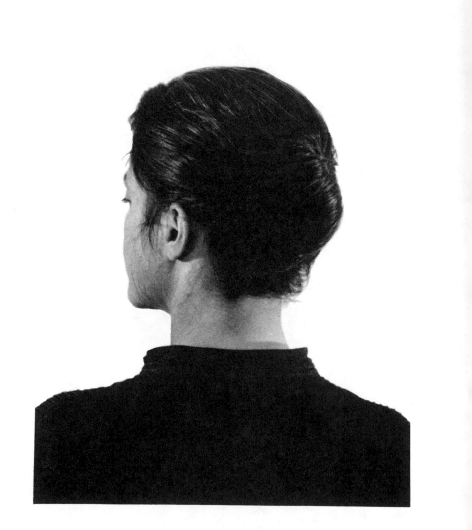

Although the French Twist is not technically a braid, it is included here because it closely resembles some of the more sophisticated braided styles. It is extremely easy to fashion; with a little practice, you'll be able to create this classic style in less than one minute.

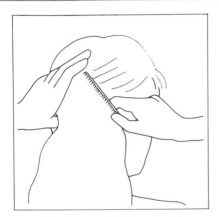

1. Comb your hair smoothly back from your forehead.

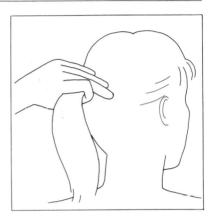

2. Gather your hair into a ponytail with a base halfway between your crown and nape and slightly to the left of center. Don't anchor it.

3. Twist the ponytail all the way around twice, in a clockwise direction. This will hold its base more closely against your head.

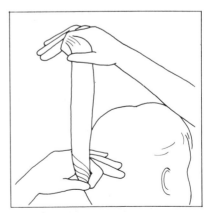

4. Hold the base of the ponytail in your left hand. With your right, hold its end up, pointing toward the ceiling.

FRENCH TWIST

Like braids, the French Twist is extremely practical. A properly fashioned French Twist will keep your hair elegantly in order all day. A successful French Twist pulls all your hair smoothly away from your face to meet in a graceful, sloping roll at the left side of the back of your head.

Like braiding, creating a French Twist requires a

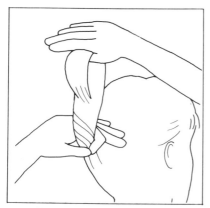

5. With your right hand, fold the end of the ponytail (about the top third) down toward your nape.

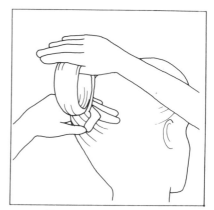

6. Fold the entire ponytail down under itself, toward your nape, so that it is less than half as long as it was.

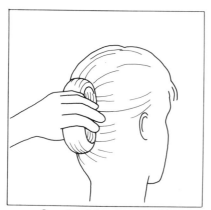

7. Cup the folded ponytail in your left hand. There should be a slight hollow between the ponytail and your scalp.

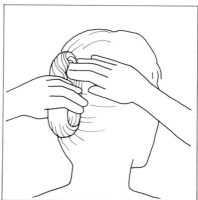

8. With your right hand, begin to gently push the upper right-hand portion of the folded ponytail down into the hollow.

combination of visualization and practice. When you look at a completed French Twist, it is difficult to imagine how it was fashioned. The step-by-step illustrations below, however, will show you how easy it is. Imagine yourself carrying out each of the steps on your own hair before you begin.

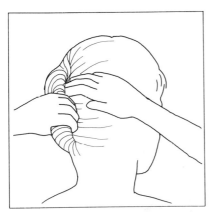

9. Continue pushing the hair underneath your left hand into the hollow, so that the folded ponytail is slowly rolling inside the hollow.

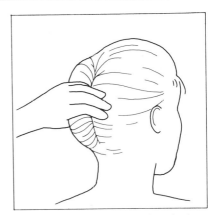

10. The twist is completed when you can't push any additional hair into the hollow, and the folded ponytail has become a tight roll.

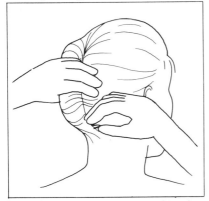

11. Create a "seam" by tucking in bobby pins along the line formed where the right hand edge of the roll meets your scalp, starting at the bottom.

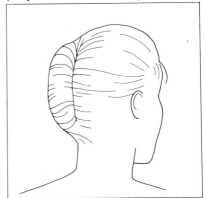

12. Place bobby pins all along the "seam," up to the top of the roll, concealing them just under the roll.

UNDERBRAID

The glamorous Underbraid appears elaborate and intricate, but it is actually just as easy to fashion as a French braid. It combines French and Dutch braiding techniques to create a stunning braid that stands out from your head, surrounded by gracefully draped hair.

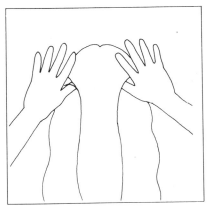

1. Place your thumbs above and behind your ears. Draw your thumbs slightly back and upward, gathering the hair that meets at your crown into a ponytail.

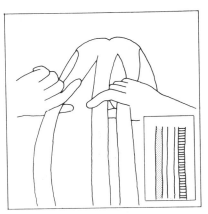

2. Divide the ponytail into three approximately equal strands and position your fingers to begin braiding.

3. Cross the left strand under the center, taking the center strand to the left.

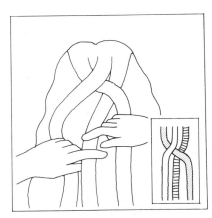

4. Cross the right strand under the center, taking the center strand to the right.

UNDERBRAID

The Underbraid is, in fact, the opposite of a French braid. Instead of hiding the braided ponytail underneath the gathers of hair, the Underbraid uses the gathered hair as a base underneath the braid, causing it to stand out.

Because the Underbraid is created using motions that may seem unfamiliar at first, it's important that you use the hand

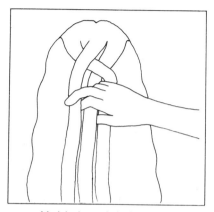

5. Hold the plait in your right hand, separating the three loose strands below it with your fingers.

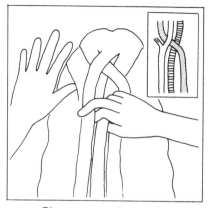

6. Place your left thumb above and slightly behind your ear. Draw a strand half as thick as one of the original strands toward the ponytail.

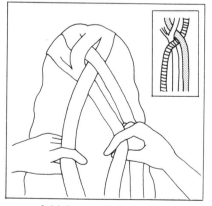

7. Add the newly gathered hair to the left strand. Cross the increased left strand under the center, taking the center strand to the left.

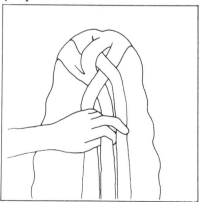

8. Hold the plait in your left hand, separating the three loose strands below it with your fingers.

positions and movements that feel most comfortable to you. These illustrations show a braider using her own individual technique. As long as you fashion one Dutch plait and then begin gathering hair and crossing the increased strands **under** the center, it really doesn't matter how you do it.

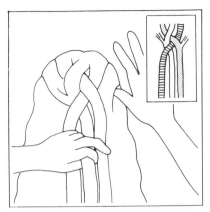

9. Use your right thumb to draw a strand about half as thick as one of the original strands toward the ponytail.

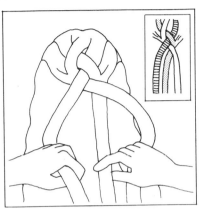

10. Add the newly gathered hair to the right strand. Cross the increased right strand under the center, taking the center strand to the right.

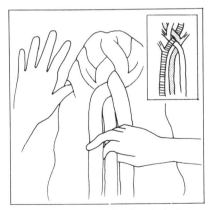

11. Continue gathering hair from the left and right and adding to the strands just before you cross them under the center.

12. When you have no loose hair left to gather, Dutch-braid the strands that are left. Fasten the end with a covered rubber band.

DRESS UP YOUR BRAIDS

Our photographs and illustrations have shown you how to create braids and braided styles; now it's up to you to experiment and add your own finishing touches. Each style we've shown can be adapted and combined with others, once you've mastered the techniques. For example, you can easily fashion two Dutch braids, one on either side of your head, by modifying the instructions given for the single Dutch braid. And, using the basic instructions, you can fashion two French braids at the back of your head or a single English braid on the side.

If you want an altogether new look, now you can add-a-braid! Available at your hair salon or by mail is a braid as long as 24" made from synthetic fiber to match any hair color. Mix and match it with your natural braids, tie it around your head, twist it into a bun, let it dangle like a pigtail. Experiment, and remember that the placement of braids is up to you.

You can also highlight your favorite braided looks with accessories. Barrettes and hair clips come in a range of colors, shapes and sizes, and even ornamented wire hairpins are widely available. They all decorate the hair they're holding. For an elegant look, try adding a delicate comb to an Invisible French braid, or pierce a braided Chignon with exotic-looking chopsticks. Also try accessories that aren't just for hair. Weave a thin strand of beads in with a Braided Face Frame, or fasten the end of an English or Dutch braid with brightly colored ribbons or yarn. The choices are yours.